SOMERSET STEAM

Scenes from the F

MICHAEL WELCH

Capital Transport

CONTENTS

Front cover: The classic view of a westbound train leaving Watchet. This illustration shows GWR Large Prairie 5101 Class locomotive No.4110 pulling away from Watchet station with the 11.40am Taunton to Minehead train on 25th August 1962 and about to tackle the 1 in 76 gradient which applied almost immediately from the platform end. After about half a mile or so the gradient eased but the incline steepened to 1 in 74 before Washford station was reached. The frontage of Watchet station can be seen on the right, whilst the vast bulk of the former Wesleyan chapel dominates the left hand side of the picture. Note the footbridge (partially concealed by steam from the engine) which links the station with the town centre and provides a short cut for many pedestrians. When the proposal was made to extend the line to Minehead the railway company proposed that the line would cross an existing road at that point on the level but the Board of Trade stipulated that a bridge must be erected a short distance westwards. The railway company was also directed to maintain the existing right of way, hence the provision of a footbridge. The Large Prairie tank locomotives were a common sight on the line in the summer months, usually being employed on the heavier trains. No.4110 survived into preservation and, at the time of writing, is being restored at Tyseley near Birmingham. *Roy Patterson*

Back cover: Lovingly maintained flower beds, a neatly manicured cutting, spotlessly clean platforms and newly repainted station furniture. The east end of Yatton station, seen here in this gem of a picture taken in 1956, has the look of a carefully prepared film set rather than a country railway junction station with hundreds of daily users. Everything seems to be just so! The station here opened on 14th June 1841 when the broad gauge line from Bristol Temple Meads to Bridgwater came into use. It was originally named Clevedon Road and renamed Yatton from 28th July 1847 when the Clevedon branch opened. The station lies on a dead straight and level section which continues southwards for seven miles. The identity of the train is unknown and, most importantly, the shot has not been marred by a dirty engine! *Colour-Rail*

Overleaf: The tower of Muchelney Abbey is just visible on the horizon as 4500 Class 2-6-2T locomotive No.4569 crosses the river Parrett with a Yeovil to Taunton train in May 1964. This location was between Langport and Thorney & Kingsbury Halt, the latter being opened on 28th November 1927 principally to serve the village of Kingsbury Episcopi. The station was, however, more than a mile from the settlement it purported to serve so is unlikely to have attracted much traffic. *Roy Hobbs*

First Published 2008

ISBN 978-1-85414-318-1

Published by Capital Transport Publishing
P.O. Box 250, Harrow, Middlesex

Printed by Fabulous Printers, Singapore

© Michael Welch 2008

Other titles in this series are:

Hampshire Steam
Sussex Steam
Kent Steam
Surrey Steam
London Steam
Dorset Steam

INTRODUCTION

Mention the county of Somerset to the average railway aficionado and the thoughts of most will immediately turn to the legendary Somerset & Dorset line (S&D). This was unquestionably an absolutely splendid route which still seems to be virtually everyone's favourite more than forty years after its sad demise. It was, perhaps, inevitable that a cross country line connecting the Georgian city of Bath with the premier resort of Bournemouth would have a high profile, but the highly individualistic S&D had much more to offer than simply the famous places at each end of the line. These included the fierce climbs over the Mendip Hills, the long straight, level stretches across the flatlands to Glastonbury, a bewildering mix of single and double line sections not to mention the quite extraordinary operating manoeuvres at Templecombe. Add to this the most remarkable assortment of motive power imaginable and some of the best countryside Great Britain has to offer and it is easy to see why it is still a much lamented line. The late Ivo Peters, the well-known S&D photographer, skilfully recorded the line in all of its moods in both monochrome and colour cine film and referred to the route's 'character and charm' which he captured brilliantly on camera. Furthermore, the S&D retained steam traction right up to the end in March 1966, far later than other Somerset lines, and this has ensured that the route's twilight years were recorded for posterity by many photographers. Often called the 'Slow and Dirty' by its detractors, your author would much prefer to remember it as 'Swift and Delightful'. Regrettably this really outstanding line finished up being 'Sabotaged and Defeated'. What a terrible shame!

It would be wrong, however, to suggest that the S&D, which in pre-grouping days was run by the London & South Western and Midland Railways under a joint leasing arrangement, was in any way typical of railways in Somerset – far from it! Many of Somerset's routes were originally built by the Bristol & Exeter Railway as broad gauge lines and these, plus other locally promoted branch lines, were later swallowed up by the Great Western Railway (GWR) which became by far the most dominant force in the county in terms of track mileage and certainly traffic density. There are two principal former GWR main lines, the Bristol to Taunton line, which today forms part of the north east to south west main traffic artery and the Westbury to Taunton line which is, of course, part of the principal passenger route from the capital to the west of England. This has a particular claim to fame, the section west of Castle Cary being one of the last stretches of main line to be constructed in Great Britain. It was opened as the GWR's 'new direct route to the West' in 1906. In times gone by these main lines carried local services which served intermediate towns and villages, as well as fast expresses, and stations with quaint sounding names like Long Sutton & Pitney, Puxton & Worle and Creech St Michael Halt still appeared on the railway map.

When harsh economic realities finally caught up with the railway industry in the early 1960s, the late Doctor (later Lord) Beeching immediately identified stopping passenger services as hopelessly uneconomic and the vast majority quickly disappeared from the timetables, those in Somerset being no exception. In addition to the former GWR lines, three separate sections of the former London & South Western Railway (LSWR) route from Waterloo to Exeter pass through Somerset but it should be noted, however, that Yeovil Junction station,

which serves a sizeable town, is actually located just over the county border in Dorset and therefore outside the scope of this volume. Despite being downgraded in importance in the mid-1960s in favour of the former GWR route, this line managed to retain a greater proportion of its local, intermediate stations and in more recent years has benefited from the reopening of some, such as Templecombe.

Like branch railways in most parts of Great Britain, Somerset's secondary lines were largely promoted by local people, very often entrepreneurs, who wished to see their town connected to the rapidly expanding national railway network to facilitate the speedier movement of goods. Some of these lines were not built as a single entity but constructed on a piecemeal basis, two classic examples being the Witham to Yatton, and Chard branches, both of which saw the initial involvement of two totally separate railway companies and, in the case of the latter, two different gauges! Many Somerset branch lines fanned out from Taunton, to Chard, Yeovil, Minehead and Barnstaple, and all had their particular characteristics. In the summer months the normally very quiet Barnstaple line, which served very few intermediate settlements of consequence, carried heavy Saturday holiday traffic due to it being the shortest route from London and the Midlands to the popular resort of Ilfracombe. In total contrast to summer Saturdays, when the line was no doubt worked almost to capacity, Sunday was very much a 'day of rest' for staff as no trains at all were timetabled. Travellers on the Chard branch had to study the timetable closely because, apart from the extremely sparse and slow service provided, unwary through passengers could be faced with long waits at Chard Town and again at Chard Junction, which was generally served only by local stopping trains on the former LSWR main line. Perhaps the most interesting branch line in many ways was the attractive 31¾ mile long Witham to Yatton line (latterly most westbound trains started at Frome) which linked a number of small settlements including Shepton Mallet, Wells and Cheddar. The latter location, like some others in Somerset, boasted an attractive overall roof, but the most fascinating spot on the line was undoubtedly Wells, where trains on the former GWR branch crossed over the tracks of the S&D goods yard on the level. Incredibly, at one time this small city was served by three stations and had two engine sheds.

Compilation of this album would not have been possible without the help and co-operation of many railway photographers who have kindly loaned their irreplaceable transparencies for publication, thus enabling them to be appreciated by a much wider audience. I would like to record my appreciation to them. Additionally, Chris Evans, David Fakes, John Langford and Graham Mallinson have scrutinised the manuscript and suggested many improvements to the text. Trevor Rapley, a colleague in the Bluebell Railway Carriage & Wagon Dept, has also assisted and thanks are also due to this gentleman. I accept responsibility for any errors that remain undetected.

M.S.W.
Burgess Hill,
West Sussex,
December 2007

FROME – CASTLE CARY – TAUNTON

A scene at Frome on 31st July 1965 showing the 10.45am Wolverhampton to Weymouth train entering the station with BR Standard Class 5MT 4-6-0 No.73018 in charge. This service ran on Saturdays only at the height of the summer season for holiday-makers. In the days before private motoring and inexpensive continental holidays became the norm for the masses, most British families spent their annual holiday at the seaside and reached their destination by rail. The dates of the annual holiday exodus were determined by the school holidays and consequently huge numbers of people were on the move to the coastal resorts in the peak months of July and August. This put a tremendous strain on the railway's resources and a large number of coaches, which were idle for most of the year, had to be retained to cater for this annual surge of passengers. This traffic was quickly identified by the late Doctor (later Lord) Beeching as hopelessly uneconomic and trains such as the one seen here were quickly removed from the timetable.
Hugh Ballantyne

The glory days of Western Region steam. In the 1950s the WR embarked on a programme of naming certain crack express services which were generally formed of the latest BR Standard coaches painted in chocolate and cream livery. The 1.30pm Paddington to Penzance and 11.05am train in the opposite direction were christened 'The Royal Duchy' in January 1957. On Mondays to Fridays these trains also conveyed a Kingswear portion. In this picture, taken on a rather wet 22nd June 1957, the down train is seen passing over Blatchbridge Junction in the care of 'Castle' Class 4-6-0 No.5020 *Trematon Castle* which is carrying an extremely prominent headboard. The line veering off to the left leads to Frome. *Colour-Rail*

The 10.30am Torquay to Paddington summer Saturday express speeds through Bruton station, also on 15th July 1961. Motive power is thought to be 'Castle' Class No.5003 *Lulworth Castle*. The attractive town is on the right of the shot. The station here is one of the few between Taunton and Westbury that remain open today, being served solely by infrequent local trains on the Weymouth to Bristol route. Note the signal box – partially visible on the left – and semaphore signalling, both of which have long since been consigned to history on this stretch of line. *John Langford*

Opposite: GWR 'Hall' Class 4-6-0 No.4996 *Eden Hall*, approaches Bruton station with (what appears to be) the 9.05am Paddington to Weymouth (via Chippenham) train on 15th July 1961. This train was booked to pass Bruton at 12.58pm. The steam visible in the distance is being emitted by No.5935 *Norton Hall*, in charge of the 11.12am Weymouth to Paddington, from which the photographer had alighted a few minutes earlier. *John Langford*

Photographed in open country west of Bruton, an unidentified 'King' 4-6-0 speeds towards London at the head of the 8.15am Perranporth to Paddington train. This was another summer Saturday working and had no advertised stops in the public timetable after leaving Par. Passengers joining the train at St Austell and Par were advised that the train 'calls to take up passengers for Paddington only'. This picture was also taken on 15th July 1961. Less than a mile from this location the GWR route passed under the Somerset & Dorset line. Bruton was actually served by two separate stations, the latter line having one called Cole for Bruton which was reasonably convenient for passengers travelling to Bruton. *John Langford*

An unidentified pannier tank locomotive gets away from Castle Cary with a local train bound for Yeovil Pen Mill on 11th May 1962. The station here dates from 1st September 1856 when the Wilts, Somerset & Weymouth Railway opened its broad gauge line from Frome to Yeovil. Conversion to standard gauge was carried out in the 1870s. At this time GWR passengers travelling between London and the West Country had to go via Bristol but in 1906 the GWR opened its 'new direct route to the west' between Castle Cary and Taunton which dramatically reduced journey times. Castle Cary became a junction station for the first time and a new signal box was built, however this was destined to have a relatively short life, being destroyed by enemy action on 3rd September 1942. It was replaced by the structure seen on the left of this shot, this lasting until February 1985 when the area went over to colour-light signalling controlled by Westbury panel box. *Alan Jarvis*

A further view of the western end of Castle Cary station showing the track layout where the (then) double track route to Yeovil diverged from the main line. Part of the signal box and goods yard are also visible, while the shot also provides an excellent detailed view of a GWR bracket signal. It should be noted that the Yeovil route was converted to single line operation from 12th May 1968 when the position of the junction was moved eastwards. An eastbound freight train is approaching the station hauled by 'County' Class 4-6-0 No.1028 *County of Warwick* and at first sight this appears to be double-headed, however, the second locomotive is pannier tank No.9497 which was being hauled 'dead' in the formation *en route* to Swindon works for scrapping. *Alan Jarvis*

Long Sutton & Pitney station was situated between Langport East and Somerton on the Castle Cary to Taunton line and is seen here in July 1962. The rather dainty and very distinctive 'pagoda' shelters, painted in GWR light and dark stone colours, were supplied in kit form by an outside contractor and used widely throughout the system. Long Sutton & Pitney was downgraded from a fully staffed station to an unstaffed halt on 26th September 1955 and was closed on 10th September 1962, at the same time as other local stations on the Castle Cary to Taunton section. *Roy Hobbs*

Passengers using Creech St Michael Halt during the summer of 1961 would have been greeted by the absolutely magnificent floral displays depicted here. This halt was located 2¾ miles east of Taunton and opened on 13th August 1928. It should be noted, however, that the line at this point was quadrupled in the early 1930s so the original station would have looked much different to that seen here. Presumably one of the original platforms, which would have been quite new at the time, had to be rebuilt in order to make way for the extra tracks. Latterly, the train service at Creech St Michael could hardly be described as brilliant. In the summer 1961 timetable there were three Monday to Friday workings to/from Castle Cary, while four services to/from Yeovil were advertised. It probably came as no surprise to local people when closure came on 5th October 1964. *John Langford*

There has been a station at Taunton since the Bristol & Exeter Railway opened their line on 1st July 1842. Originally, both up and down platforms were placed end to end on the south side of the line, but as traffic increased the operational limitations of this arrangement became apparent; the premises underwent a major rebuilding in 1868 when a more conventional layout with the up and down platforms opposite each other was adopted and a 200 feet-long train shed was built. The platforms were extended in 1895. In the 1930s the lines from Cogload Junction to Norton Fitzwarren were widened from two to four tracks and this work prompted another rebuilding of the station, this time involving demolition of the train shed and construction of an island platform so that each of the four through tracks was served by a platform. At the same time a new subway was built together with a booking office on the north side of the line. The following selection of pictures gives some idea of the locomotive types that could be seen at Taunton during steam's twilight years. When they were introduced in 1927 the GWR 'King' Class 4-6-0s were the most powerful locomotives in Great Britain, but when this portrait of No.6019 *King Henry V* working a Plymouth to Paddington train was taken on 8th September 1962 the class was very much on the way out and, indeed, No.6019 was withdrawn later the same month. Sadly, the entire class had been condemned by the end of the year: all the 'Kings' had been deposed. *Colin Caddy*

A summer Saturday holiday train from Ilfracombe is seen at Taunton on the same day as the previous shot. Class 4300 2-6-0 No.7337, which is in quite presentable external condition, simmers gently while waiting to be removed from the train in favour of a larger 'Hall' class engine. The *ex*-LMSR coaches suggest that this may have been heading for a destination on the London Midland Region. *Colin Caddy*

The up 'Torbay Express' pauses at Taunton with immaculate 'Castle' Class 4-6-0 No.7022 *Hereford Castle* in charge. The locomotive certainly seems to be attracting the attention of some spotters on the platform. This picture was also taken on 8th September 1962. This train ran between Paddington and Kingswear. No.7022 was built at Swindon in 1949 and survived to become one of the very last 'Castle' class engines in traffic, not being withdrawn until June 1965. *Colin Caddy*

This portrait of 4300 Class 2-6-0 No.7303 standing at one of Taunton station's up platforms was taken in 1964, by which time steam traction was very much in decline in the area. This machine was withdrawn in September 1964 so the picture was presumably taken before that time. It is likely that the 'Mogul' had just brought in a train off the Barnstaple line. This shot shows the platform canopies and associated structures that dated from the rebuilding undertaken in 1932. The canopies on the island platform were subsequently removed and the platform taken out of regular use. Some years ago, however, the island platform returned to use. *Colour-Rail*

BRISTOL TO FROME

The expansion of the Somerset coalfield in the late 18th century required many transport links, one of the first being the Somerset Coal Canal, opened in 1798. In the middle of the 19th century the first railways reached the West Country and this form of transport seemed the ideal method of moving bulk commodities such as coal. The Wiltshire, Somerset & Weymouth Railway (WS&WR) reached Frome in 1850 but soon afterwards was taken over by the GWR. The single track, broad gauge Frome to Radstock branch was completed on 14th November 1854 to serve the many collieries in the Radstock area. The line onwards from Radstock to Bristol opened as a standard gauge route in 1873 and included a sixteen arch, 995 feet-long viaduct over the river Chew at Pensford. In June 1874 the GWR converted the Frome to Radstock section to standard gauge. The first, direct passenger trains from Bristol to Frome ran on 5th July 1875. In its heyday twenty-five coal mines and four stone quarries were connected to the line and in addition to this traffic milk was also conveyed. It is recorded that in 1911 a total of 32,539 churns were despatched from Mells Road station alone. Passenger trains ceased on 2nd November 1959, the Radstock to Bristol section being subsequently abandoned. The final coal train, from Writhlington pit, ran on 16th November 1973. The line to Radstock remained in use until 1988, however, to give access to a wagon repair works, the last section of all in use being the stretch from Frome to Whatley quarry. This view of Pensford station was taken on 22nd August 1959. *Alan Jarvis*

Over the years many pictures of the other Radstock station, on the Somerset & Dorset line, have appeared in a variety of publications but here, for a change, is a shot of a train at Radstock West station. This photograph depicts a Bristol to Frome train, headed by GWR 0-6-0 pannier tank locomotive No.9615, a Swindon product constructed in September 1945. The engine is seen taking water during its stop at Radstock, also on 22nd August 1959. Passenger services along the line were never lavish; in 1910, for example, there were only eight trains along the Bristol to Radstock section and not all of those continued to Frome. In the 1920s two halts were opened, at Whitchurch and Farrington Gurney, in order to stimulate traffic but clearly they were not entirely successful. *Alan Jarvis*

On Saturday 24th February 1962 the photographer was a participant on a Railway Enthusiasts Club, of Farnborough, Hampshire, brake van trip from Bristol East depot to Radstock West, Frome and Westbury. By that date the Bristol to Frome line had been freight-only for some years and no doubt he hoped to obtain one or two pictures along the way. The club members were conveyed in a brake van next to the engine, the train as far as Radstock comprising of 26 empty mineral wagons. From the photographers' point of view, however, that part of the journey was a bit of a disaster because not only was the locomotive bunker first but the train only made two very brief halts *en route* neither of which provided an opportunity for photography. On arrival at Radstock the participants were greeted by this incredibly busy scene (for a Saturday morning!), the yard almost overflowing with wagons, Radstock being the centre of the local coal industry at that time. The locomotive on the left is 5101 Class 2-6-2T No.4131, which had earlier powered the train from Bristol, while in the middle of the picture is 0-6-0PT No.3614, the engine that later took the party on to Westbury. The line on the right was a connection with the adjacent S&D line via Ludlow's colliery sidings, but it should be noted that this was never used by regular traffic. *John Langford*

Frome station on 20th June 1959 showing 5700 Class pannier tank locomotive No.3614 standing in the down platform presumably after arrival with a train from Bristol. The distinctive station buildings include an overall roof with a clerestory window which runs the full length of the ridge. The premises were originally built for the Wiltshire, Somerset & Weymouth Railway and date from 1850, though it should be noted that this company had been taken over by the GWR by the time the station opened. The timber roof is 120 feet long, 48 feet wide and the hipped roof consists of twelve composite trusses supported by square timber columns. No.3614 entered service in March 1939 and lasted until March 1962. *Colour-Rail*

BATH SPA STATION

During the 1960s the attention of many steam enthusiasts was focussed upon the immensely popular Somerset & Dorset line which remained an oasis of steam power, in an area largely operated by diesel traction, right up to its closure in March 1966. It is, perhaps, for this reason that few photographs of Bath Spa station were submitted for inclusion in this album, despite the fact that it was much busier than the neighbouring Green Park station on the S&D line. Seen against a splendid background of Georgian terraces and wooded hillsides, the 5.25pm Salisbury to Cardiff train is depicted arriving at Bath Spa in superb evening sunshine on 28th August 1961. Motive power is a beautifully turned out 'Hall' Class 4-6-0 No.5903 *Keele Hall*, a Swindon product (where else?) built in May 1931. It was eventually withdrawn from service in September 1963. *Hugh Ballantyne*

The 5.25pm Salisbury to Cardiff train is seen again, this time on 30th April 1963. In this portrait the train is pulling away from its Bath Spa station stop with another very clean 'Hall' Class locomotive in charge. On this occasion the locomotive was No.6944 *Fledborough Hall*. The circular signal on the extreme left of the picture is a banner repeater signal which gave engine drivers an early indication of the aspect shown by the next signal. Banner repeaters were installed where a signal was partially obscured (in this case by the station canopy) or relatively poorly sited. *Hugh Ballantyne*

WITHAM TO YATTON

The branch line from Witham to Yatton was not planned as a single undertaking but constructed by two completely separate companies, the East Somerset Railway (ESR) and the Bristol & Exeter Railway (B&ER). The inaugural meeting of the East Somerset Railway took place in Shepton Mallet on 29th September 1855 and a broad gauge line was proposed to connect with the Wiltshire, Somerset & Weymouth Railway at Witham. This scheme was approved by Parliament on 5th June 1856, a contract to the value of £64,400 was signed with Rowland Brotherhood of Chippenham, and work commenced on 1st April 1857. The line opened to Shepton Mallet on 9th November 1858, the first train apparently being hauled by a GWR 4-4-0ST named *Homer*. In response to pressure from local people an extension to Wells was approved and services commenced on 28th February 1862. This was the second station in the city, the Somerset Central Railway (SCR) having opened an extension from Glastonbury in 1859. The stations were very close to each other on opposite sides of Priory Road. The B&ER section from Yatton to Cheddar was brought into use on 3rd August 1869, the continuation to Wells Tucker Street station opening on 5th April 1870. The ESR and B&ER became part of the GWR in the mid-1870s, and by 1876 both lines had been converted to standard gauge and linked together, but the Board of Trade objected to through passenger running because trains had to cross the SCR goods yard on the level. Through passenger working eventually commenced between the former ESR and B&ER lines in 1878. The passenger service provided on the branch was sparse: for example in the summer 1961 timetable only six weekday trains were advertised between Yatton and Wells of which a mere four continued onwards to Witham. Closure to passenger traffic occurred on 9th September 1963 but ballast workings still survive at the time of writing from Merehead quarry. The unpretentious station buildings at Witham, looking towards Frome, are seen in this picture which was taken some time in the early 1960s. *J.H. Moss/Stuart Ackley collection*

'Witham junction for Shepton Mallet and Wells' proclaims the running-in board at the western end of Witham station's up platform. In the summer of 1961 at least some branch trains started or terminated their journeys at either Frome or Westbury, so it is likely that passengers from London would have changed there rather than at Witham (which served only the tiny village of Witham Friary) where facilities were somewhat limited, to say the least. In this picture the quite complicated layout at the western end of Witham station can be clearly seen, with the line towards Wells prominent on a high embankment in the background on the right of the picture. The goods yard and signal box are on the left while the bay platform for branch trains to Wells is on the right. Part of the bay used to be covered by a rather ornate overall roof which survived at least until the mid-1950s. Witham station remained open for some time after the withdrawal of the branch service in September 1963, eventually closing from 3rd October 1966.
J.H. Moss/Stuart Ackley collection

An everyday scene at Cranmore station, thought to have been taken in the early 1960s. Note the neat and tidy appearance of the station. The fireman of 5700 Class pannier tank locomotive No.3696, hauling a westbound train, collects the single line token from the signalman, while a train bound for Frome waits in the other platform. The layout dated from 1904 when a new down platform was built alongside an existing siding and a new signalbox was erected on the down side replacing the old box on the platform. Today Cranmore is well known as the headquarters of the preserved East Somerset Railway. *Colour-Rail*

The remarkable popularity of the S&D line meant that other lines in Somerset tended to be overshadowed. It is, perhaps, for this reason that pictures of Shepton Mallet Charlton Road station are commonplace, whereas colour photographs of the town's High Street station are much rarer. This picture was taken at the latter station on the very last day of services between Witham and Yatton, 7th September 1963, the branch remaining predominately steam-worked to the end, although Type 2 diesels had one regular turn. In this shot the 2.45pm Yatton to Frome train has just arrived at Shepton Mallet behind Collett 2251 Class 0-6-0 No.3218, while the 3.28pm in the opposite direction can be seen waiting in the up platform with BR Standard Class 3MT 2-6-2T No.82037 in charge. The last Yatton to Witham train was worked by No.2268, while pannier tank locomotive No.3696 performed on the final passenger working of all, the 8.20pm from Yatton to Wells. *Hugh Ballantyne*

A fascinating picture of part of the layout at Wells looking eastwards towards the former GWR engine shed which can just be discerned in the distance. The principal running line is in the middle of the photograph while a mound of earth on the left marks the site of the ESR station. The latter was used only for a very brief period before ESR trains started to use the Somerset Central Railway's premises which were located just a few yards away on the other side of Priory Road. The locomotive depot was a sub shed of Bristol (Bath Road) and had no allocation of its own nor maintenance facilities, being merely an overnight stabling point. *Colour-Rail*

Wells has considerable claim to fame as the smallest city in England, but not so widely known is the fact that at one time it boasted the terminal stations of no less than three separate railway companies. These were the Somerset Central Railway and the East Somerset Railway stations, both of which were located in Priory Road, while the Bristol & Exeter Railway's premises were located in Tucker Street. These three stations were all within a few hundred yards of each other and eventually they were all linked together. By the late-1950s only Tucker Street remained operational and in this rare view a train to Witham is seen awaiting departure behind 5700 Class 0-6-0PT No.8790 on the glorious day of 29th August 1959. Note the very large space between the platforms indicating that the line was originally built as a broad gauge route. Following the withdrawal of passenger services in September 1963 goods traffic from Witham lingered on until April 1969. *David Soggee*

Cheddar station, looking eastwards on 4th August 1962, with BR Standard Class 3MT 2-6-2T No.82040 waiting in the platform with a train bound for Yatton. A total of 45 of these machines was built at Swindon for light passenger work, this particular example entering traffic in May 1955. It had an active life of just over ten years, being withdrawn in July 1965. Cheddar station retained much of its B&ER atmosphere until the end, the two platforms being widely spaced, this being a relic of broad gauge days. The signal box, located at the end of the up platform, was the original B&ER cabin. The station's overall roof was latterly in a poor structural condition and had to be propped up in the middle. Cheddar's main industries which brought business to the railway were strawberry growing and tourists and during the fruit picking season special trains conveying strawberries were run, a special fleet of vans being retained for this traffic. Sadly, by the date of this picture most tourists, who flocked to the town to see the famous gorge and caves, had turned their backs on the railway in favour of road transport. After the withdrawal of passenger trains goods workings continued from Yatton to Cheddar until 1st October 1964. *Colour-Rail*

A nicely turned out Ivatt-designed Class 2MT 2-6-2T, No.41202, pauses at Axbridge with a train from Yatton to Witham some time in the late 1950s. No.41202, built at Crewe in December 1946, was one of the very few members of its class to carry its pre-nationalisation number. Axbridge station's solid looking signal box is clearly visible on the right. The Mendip hills, which rise to a height of almost 800 feet in the Axbridge area, are also visible on the right of the picture. *Colour-Rail*

The last station before trains reached the main line junction at Yatton was Congresbury. In this portrait a three-coach westbound train is seen pulling in to the station some time in the late 1950s. There was a small goods yard here, complete with a stone-built shed which, on the day of this photograph, contained what appears to be a rather fine clerestory coach. Note the width of the goods shed's arch, which bears testament to the line's broad gauge origins. The signalman, part of whose box is visible above the first coach, is strolling down the platform ready to exchange tokens with the driver. The line veering off to the left in the background is the former Wrington Vale Light Railway branch, opened on 14th April 1901, which terminated at Blagdon. This line, which followed a winding course, boasted four passenger trains daily in its heyday but this number had dwindled to two by the late 1920s and these were withdrawn altogether on 14th September 1931. Goods traffic continued until November 1950 when it was cut back to Wrington. In order to reflect its enhanced status as a junction, Congresbury station had a second platform and a loop added prior to the opening of the Blagdon branch. *Colour-Rail*

A further picture of Congresbury, this time showing the train seen in the previous illustration leaving with GWR 4575 Class 2-6-2T No.5528 in charge. The train is about to pass under the main A370 Bristol to Weston-super-Mare road, which today crosses the site of the line on the level. Note the strange signalling arrangements which were presumably a legacy of the days before the second platform was added. *Colour-Rail*

'Yatton – Junction for Cheddar Line and Clevedon' reads the running-in board on the left, a reminder of the days when Yatton was still a fairly busy junction station. Trains to or from Witham normally used the down bay platform at Yatton and in this illustration 5700 Class pannier tank locomotive No.3702 is depicted waiting to depart with the 2.45pm to Witham on 17th August 1963. The station appears to be quite a hive of activity with a small group of passengers apparently waiting for a down train while the signalman has 'pulled off' for a diesel multiple unit in the up bay which is about to depart to Clevedon. On the right Collett 2251 Class 0-6-0 No.2268 waits between duties. *Hugh Ballantyne*

THE LSWR MAIN LINE

Three separate sections of the former LSWR main line pass through Somerset, the first being a short stretch around Templecombe, whilst the second section was much longer and extended from Yeovil Junction to about five miles beyond Crewkerne. A short stretch around Chard Junction is also in Somerset. In this portrait a westbound express is seen running into Templecombe station on 1st September 1962 behind Bulleid 'Battle of Britain' Class Pacific No.34074 *46 Squadron*, which was one of the first to be withdrawn and is reputed to be the least photographed Light Pacific – at least in colour! The Somerset & Dorset line to Bournemouth passed beneath the SR main line in front of the water tank, the bridge railings just being visible.
Alan Jarvis

The 8.25am Plymouth to Waterloo train, with Bulleid Pacific No.34060 *25 Squadron* in charge, awaits departure from Templecombe on 27th July 1963. When the S&D line was closed in March 1966 Templecombe station was shut at the same time and subsequently razed to the ground, leaving only the signal box standing. This orgy of destruction was particularly regrettable because the station was relatively modern, being built in the typical Southern Railway style of the 1930s, and the premises even boasted the luxury of a refreshment room. Following closure considerable development took place in the area and pressure from local people eventually succeeded in obtaining an experimental reopening in 1983. The reopening was extremely successful, but what a pity the original station canopies are no longer there to shield passengers from the wind and rain, nor the cosy buffet to provide a sanctuary on a cold morning. *Hugh Ballantyne*

A further view of Templecombe, this time depicting the west end of the station, where the large signal box was situated. The trains are unidentified, but the one on the left, standing in the platform used by Somerset & Dorset line trains, is likely to be the summer Saturday Cleethorpes to Exmouth through service. This was a fascinating working which was, in effect, two trains combined into one, the purpose of the first part of its journey being to convey homebound holiday-makers from Cleethorpes, while after departure from Birmingham the atmosphere on the train was, no doubt, rather different as it took outgoing holiday-makers to their fortnight by the sea on the south Devon coast. One wonders how many passengers appreciated the fact that the booked motive power, apparently, for the last leg of the journey from Templecombe was nothing larger than a Maunsell 'Mogul', the reason for this presumably being the shortage of larger locomotives on a busy summer Saturday. Here, N Class No.31855 is seen waiting to leave on 1st September 1962 with the crew probably not relishing the task of taking such a heavy train over Honiton bank. The train on the down main line appears to be a local stopping service with BR Standard Class 5MT No.73088 *Joyous Gard* in charge. *Alan Jarvis*

In September 1964 the Western Region took over operation of the Waterloo to Exeter line which involved the withdrawal of through services to stations west of Exeter and the introduction of a new, diesel-hauled semi-fast service. Steam aficionados mourned the loss of the steam-hauled workings on this route, including the famous 'Atlantic Coast Express', which had become the fastest train scheduled to be worked by steam traction in Great Britain. No doubt to the surprise and delight of many enthusiasts, who probably thought they would never again travel behind steam over Honiton bank on a normal service train, steam re-appeared on the route in the summer of 1965 working various Saturday extra trains. In this picture the 11.15am Exmouth to Waterloo is seen approaching Templecombe on 17th July 1965 with No.34006 *Bude* in charge.
John Beckett

One of the things that used to make the study of railways so absorbing was the proliferation of 'odd' cross-country services that often did not fit in with the regular pattern of services along a certain route. One such train was the Plymouth to Brighton/Portsmouth (and vice versa) train which was routed via Okehampton, the West of England main line as far as Salisbury and then along the coast to Brighton. In this photograph Bulleid 'West Country' Class Pacific No.34015 *Exmouth* is shown entering Crewkerne station with the 11.10am *ex*-Plymouth on 11th April 1964.
Hugh Ballantyne

'Chard Junction – Change for Chard' proudly states the informative green running-in board at Chard Junction station in this picture which was taken on 28th April 1962. In the summer 1957 timetable on the main line Chard Junction was largely served by slow, infrequent stopping trains with variable connections for Chard Central. Some of these involved long waits, hardly an inviting prospect on a wet and windy night, so it is unlikely that a change of train at Chard Junction would have been the preferred option for many people travelling to Chard. Chard Junction was a victim of the Western Region's 'rationalisation' of the stations on the Salisbury to Exeter line, closing in March 1966. *Roy Patterson*

This photograph of Chard Junction station and its environs was taken looking eastwards from the goods yard on 25th June 1961. The physical connection between the main and branch lines was achieved through the goods yard line on the extreme left which was not used for ordinary passenger traffic, although it could be used in exceptional circumstances. The small yellow-painted building immediately to the left of the roadway was originally a signal box that controlled movements on the branch, but it was reduced to the status of a ground frame in March 1935. When the line north of Chard Central was closed to freight traffic on 6th July 1964 all freight movements were handled from Chard Junction, but even this came to an end in October 1966 when the last remnant of the branch was closed and all the rails had been lifted by the end of December 1967. The first section of the branch to be built thus became the last part to be closed. Note the wagon just creeping into the picture on the right. This appears to be a milk tank, movement of this commodity being at one time a substantial source of revenue from the dairy on the down side of the line. Despite closure of the station, the loop remains in regular operation for passing trains on the single line. *John Langford*

YEOVIL TOWN TO YEOVIL JUNCTION

A view of Yeovil Town station on 3rd December 1963 showing Bulleid 'West Country' Class Pacific No.34107 *Blandford Forum* simmering in the station, presumably after arrival from Yeovil Junction. Like the vast majority of these machines No.34107 was built at Brighton Works from where it emerged in April 1950. Unfortunately, *Blandford Forum* was a victim of the WR's purge of Southern steam power which occurred in September 1964 following the dieselisation of the Waterloo to Exeter service. *Alan Reeve*

When the WR assumed control of former Southern territory west of Salisbury in 1963 they soon started to 'Westernise' operations, although some cynics might say, for some lines at least, that really meant closure was just around the corner. For many years the shuttle service linking Yeovil Junction and Town stations was provided in the traditional Southern manner by a push-pull train, latterly worked by an M7 Class 0-4-4T. In this shot No.30131 is seen standing between duties at Yeovil Town station on 1st September 1962. The rolling stock consists of two Maunsell coaches converted for push-pull operation, the far vehicle having being specially modified with a cab for the driver. *Colin Caddy*

The M7 Class locomotives and Southern 'push-pull' coaches were ousted by GWR pannier tank engines working auto coaches in March 1963 and in this picture No.5416 is also depicted at Yeovil Town station. This shot was taken on 23rd March 1963. No.5416 was a 5400 Class engine, one of 25 constructed at Swindon in the 1930s to replace older pannier tank locomotives that were fitted for push-pull operation. No.5416 was built in June 1932 and lasted in traffic for a further five months after this picture was taken. The class was rendered extinct when the last survivors were withdrawn in October 1963. *Colin Caddy*

BR Standard Class 9F 2-10-0 No.92001 makes an energetic departure from Bath (Green Park) with the 7.45am SO Bradford Forster Square to Bournemouth train on 15th July 1961. The train is approaching Bath Junction signal box (where the S&D route diverged from the line to Mangotsfield) and note the 9F's fireman has extended the tablet catcher so the tablet for the single-line section to Midford can be collected from the lineside apparatus. Locomotives of this class revolutionised the working of heavy Saturday holiday trains over the S&D line following their introduction during the summer of 1960 – they were permitted to take 410 tons unassisted – and four members of the class were allocated to Bath shed especially for this traffic. The 9Fs were only based on the S&D during the summer because they were not fitted with steam heating equipment and consequently the engines involved changed from year to year. Nos.92000/1/6 and 92212 were the locomotives allocated to the S&D during the summer of 1961. Note the 'Jinty' 0-6-0T shunting on the right. *Hugh Ballantyne*

Photographed on a beautiful early spring afternoon, the 4.37pm Bath to Templecombe train slows for the Midford station stop on 27th March 1965. Motive power is BR Standard Class 4MT 4-6-0 No.75072, this being one of three locomotives of this class (the others being Nos.75071 and 75073) allocated to Bath (Green Park) shed in the late-1950s. Between Bath and Midford trains threaded Devonshire and Combe Down tunnels, both being single bore with tight clearances and no ventilation. This made them extremely unpleasant for footplate crews, especially for enginemen on the second locomotive of a double-headed train. *Hugh Ballantyne*

The S&D line was famous for the really remarkable locomotive combinations that could be seen, particularly on summer Saturdays when many additional holiday trains were run and locomotive resources were considerably stretched. Here an unidentified northbound express approaches Midford behind *ex*-LMSR Class 2P 4-4-0 No.40700 piloting Bulleid 'West Country' Class No.34041 *Wilton*. The pilot engine would almost certainly have been attached at Evercreech Junction to assist the Pacific over the Mendip hills. The Gresley-designed Eastern Region coaching stock suggests that the train was probably heading for Bradford or Leeds. This picture was taken in July 1961. *Colour-Rail*

Between Bath and Radstock the S&D line passed through some of the most delightful pastoral scenery to be found in north Somerset, and in this view the Cleethorpes to Exmouth Saturdays-only through train is depicted heading southwards from Midford. The line pursued a sinuous course on this stretch because it followed the remains of the Somerset coal canal. Motive power is former S&D 2-8-0 No.53806 piloted by BR Standard Class 4MT 4-6-0 No.75009 and this photograph was taken on 25th August 1962. Earlier the latter engine had piloted a Class 9F on the northbound 'Pines Express' so it had a particularly busy day. *Alan Jarvis*

Radstock was the centre of the north Somerset coalfield and the source of a great deal of railborne freight traffic. Pictured against a stunning background of autumn colours BR Standard Class 5MT 4-6-0 No.73092 is seen shunting at Writhlington on 31st October 1964. There was a colliery located here, which was closed in 1973, the area around Radstock being characterised by colliery winding gear and pit heaps, a totally different environment to the rest of the largely rural S&D line. No.73092 was allocated to Bath (Green Park) shed at the time of this photograph but later found sanctuary on the Southern Region where it lasted right until the end of steam traction in July 1967. The engine's green livery is well protected by a liberal covering of grime! *Alan Reeve*

The last day of public passenger services over the S&D line was 5th March 1966 and many local people plus railway enthusiasts gathered to observe and travel upon the final trains. Their spirits may have been partially lifted by the impressive sight of two immaculate Bulleid Pacifics that had been rostered to haul one of the farewell specials. The rail tour started in London, being hauled from Waterloo to Templecombe by 'Merchant Navy' Pacific No.35028 *Clan Line*. The train was then worked to Highbridge, and back as far as Evercreech Junction, by a couple of Ivatt Class 2MT 2-6-2Ts. From Evercreech the special was taken over the Mendips by Nos.34006 *Bude* and 34057 *Biggin Hill* which were turned upon arrival at Bath before departing back to Templecombe, where *Clan Line* took over for the run back to the capital. Luckily, from mid-morning onwards it had been an absolutely glorious winter's day with barely a cloud in the sky and when the Pacifics left Bath the afternoon lighting was at its best. Here the brace of Bulleids presents a truly magnificent spectacle as they leave Chilcompton tunnel on that fateful day, a sight that will, no doubt, be etched forever on the memories of those bystanders who were present. *Charles Whetmath*

Photographed in splendid soft autumn lighting conditions, S&D Class 7F 2-8-0 No.53808 grinds uphill towards Masbury summit with the Locomotive Club of Great Britain's 'Somerset & Dorset' rail tour on 30th September 1962. This train started at Waterloo behind the inevitable Bulleid Pacific and was routed to Broadstone via Ringwood. No.53808 took over for the run to Evercreech Junction, from where passengers were conveyed to Burnham-on-Sea (no less!) and return by GWR 0-6-0 No.3210. When the train got back to Evercreech No.53808 was in charge once again for the run over the Mendip hills to Bath from where No.44558, an S&D engine built in 1922, conveyed the participants to Bristol Temple Meads. A GWR 4700 Class 2-8-0 was the motive power onward to Didcot from where a 'County' Class 4-6-0 was in command to Paddington, thus finishing off what must have been a superb day out. *John Beckett*

BR Standard Class 5MT 4-6-0 No.73051 coasts downhill towards Shepton Mallet with an unidentified working – probably a pigeon special – on 18th August 1962: the gradient at this point is 1 in 50 in favour of down trains. This section of the S&D (which was opened in 1874) was originally built as a single line and doubled in 1892 and the train has just emerged from the original 242 yards-long bore. When doubling occurred the engineers realised that considerable savings could be made on tunnelling costs by using a slightly different course, the tunnel on the later section of line being only 132 yards in length. In times past there were no fewer than three quarries in the immediate area of Winsor Hill, the erstwhile Downside quarry being served by a trailing connection in the right foreground. The connection was removed in about 1940. No.73051 was one of three members of the class allocated to Bath (Green Park) shed in 1954 and remained there all its working life. *Alan Chandler*

Cole, between Evercreech Junction and Templecombe, is the location of this picture which shows BR Standard Class 9F 2-10-0 No.92233 taking the 7.45am Bradford (Forster Square) to Bournemouth West through the station on 18th August 1962. Cole station may not have been the largest on the S&D line, but it was of considerable historical significance because it was where the tracks of the Dorset Central and Somerset Central railway companies met, soon afterwards amalgamating to form the Somerset & Dorset Railway. In later years the station enjoyed considerable traffic from schools in the nearby town of Bruton. Note the person perched atop the bracket signal. He is the legendary photographer the late Ivo Peters, who lived in Bath and specialised in photographing the wonderful S&D line. He seemed to have a special gift for capturing the atmosphere of this splendid route in all of its moods, in particular the quality of his cine films of the line, at least in the author's opinion, being excellent. *Colour-Rail*

The last weekend of services on the S&D line, as previously mentioned, saw a flurry of rail tours over the route, two of which were long distance trips from London. The tour organised by the Stephenson Locomotive Society was a more modest affair, which started from Bath and travelled down to Bournemouth and back behind BR Standard Class 4MT 2-6-4T No.80043 piloted by Class 8F 2-8-0 No.48706. This ran on Sunday 6th March and the train is seen here accelerating away from Templecombe with the LSWR main line just visible behind the trees in the background. There was normally no Sunday service along the line which was specially opened to give enthusiasts a final glimpse of this famous route before its official closure from the following day. *Charles Whetmath*

The selection of pictures taken on the S&D line concludes with a couple of photographs of the Evercreech Junction to Highbridge branch. In this portrait a rather grimy former-GWR Collett 2251 Class 0-6-0, No.2218, is seen leaving West Pennard with the 4.0pm Highbridge to Evercreech Junction train on 28th August 1964. The signal box was presumably 'switched out' at the time of this picture and the train is, perhaps unusually, departing from the up platform. This was the last crossing place before Evercreech and also the point where westbound trains started their journey across the flat Somerset countryside to Glastonbury, a section of line between the two points running dead straight for four miles. There was a substantially built stone goods shed at West Pennard, the goods yard being equipped with a seven-ton hand crane. Like other stations on the Highbridge branch, West Pennard was rather remote from the small settlement it purported to serve, the village being two miles away. *Alan Reeve*

A veteran 3F Class 0-6-0, No.43216, pauses at Glastonbury and Street station with an afternoon train to Evercreech Junction on 5th August 1961. A feature of the line at this time was the regular summer Saturday passenger workings along the otherwise freight-only branch from Highbridge to Burnham-on-Sea, which were ordinary branch timetabled services specially extended to Burnham for day trippers. The train seen here was the return working of one of these special excursions. No.43216 was built by Neilson & Co. Ltd. in 1902 for the Somerset & Dorset Joint Railway and came into LMSR stock in 1930. It was withdrawn from service in September 1962. *David Soggee*

BRISTOL TO TAUNTON

A rather dirty unidentified 'Hall' Class 4-6-0 approaches Yatton with an up train on 14th September 1963. This illustration provides a comprehensive view of the track layout at the west end of the station where the Cheddar Valley line diverged to the left and the Clevedon branch went off to the right. Both of these routes had their own bay platforms, the former having a run round loop whilst the latter, which had an overall roof until 1956, was only a single line. There was a small goods yard on the down side, whilst a one-road engine shed, accessed from the Clevedon branch platform, was on the up side. The shed was closed from 7th August 1960. The very ornate and sizeable signal cabin is the 129-lever frame Yatton West box, which controlled the entire station layout. This box is the original Bristol & Exeter Railway structure. There were up and down relief lines on each side of Yatton, the down relief road being visible in the picture on the left, while the up relief line passed behind the signal box. Another signal box was located east of the station and this governed the connections to the other relief lines. *Alan Jarvis*

The railway arrived in Weston-super-Mare in 1841, the first station being a very modest affair served by a single track branch off the Bristol to Bridgwater main line. In 1866 this was superseded by a larger terminal constructed on adjacent land. Both of these were broad gauge stations, but in 1875 an additional rail was laid thus enabling standard gauge trains to reach the town for the first time. In 1875 the B&ER obtained an Act of Parliament to construct a new loop line through the town, but nine years elapsed before it was brought into use on 1st March 1884. A brand new station, later known as Weston-super-Mare General, came into use on the same date. This consisted of two through platforms and a bay at the east end, the up and down sides of the station being connected by a particularly attractive footbridge that also provided a public right of way between roads on each side of the station. This picture shows an eastbound train easing out of the station probably some time in the early 1960s: the bay platform is on the right of the shot. In the 1961 working timetable train number 1M87 was the 8.00am SO Paignton to Manchester Victoria which called at Weston-super-Mare at 10.00am. *J. H. Moss/Stuart Ackley collection*

Photographed from the Bristol end of the down platform at Weston-super-Mare General, 'Hall' Class 4-6-0 No.4947 *Nanhoran Hall* waits in the up platform in August 1960. Built in October 1929, No.4947 lasted in service until September 1962. The far platform is part of Locking Road station which was separate from the main station. *Colour-Rail*

The locomotive shed at Weston-super-Mare had a lowly status as one of four sub-sheds of Bristol Bath Road depot, but surely this tall and quite impressive building with neatly patterned, symmetrical stonework and a fancy archway deserved more? In contrast, on the right (what appears to be) a collection of wooden sheds suffices for the passenger facilities of the Locking Road excursion station. The engine shed was sandwiched between the two stations together with carriage sidings. *Colour-Rail*

A portrait of 'Modified Hall' 6959 Class No.6977 *Grundisburgh Hall* standing in the sidings at Weston-super-Mare in 1961. These locomotives were Hawksworth's development of the earlier series of 'Hall' Class engines; the first twelve machines appeared during the Second World War and the class eventually numbered seventy-one examples. No.6977 entered service in November 1947 and lasted until December 1963. In the background of this picture one of Locking Road station's running-in boards can be clearly seen. This station was opened in 1914 to cater for summer excursion traffic and remained in use until 1964. *Colour-Rail*

A particularly interesting feature of the Bristol to Taunton line occurred at Highbridge where the single track of the Somerset & Dorset line's branch to Burnham-on-Sea crossed the former GWR main line at a 45 degree angle on the level. By the time of this photograph, 16th July 1960, regular passenger trains to Burnham were very much a thing of the past, but the line was still open for freight and occasional Saturday excursions during the summer months. This picture provides an excellent view of the unusual track layout at this point together with appropriate signalling which involved both GWR lower and SR upper quadrant signals. Note especially the brightly painted signals at the platform end that were pivoted in the centre due to the confined space. Beyond the road overbridge Highbridge goods depot can be clearly seen with a northbound freight train perhaps waiting for a fast passenger working to overtake. *John Langford*

Photographed in splendid late afternoon lighting conditions, a Bristol to Taunton stopping train powered by 'Hall' Class 4-6-0 No.5995 *Wick Hall* approaches Brent Knoll station in May 1960. The wayside station here, which was served by a mere handful of trains, was still open at the time of this picture but was closed from 4th January 1971. Bleadon Hill forms the backdrop to this shot. Most WR main line motive power was maintained in quite reasonable external condition at that time, but here is an exception to the rule! Oh dear, No.5995 is absolutely filthy! A Swindon product dating from January 1940, *Wick Hall* lasted in traffic until April 1963. *The late J.H. Moss/Colour-Rail*

Unfortunately, no photographs of main line steam activity at Bridgwater were submitted for publication in this album but by way of compensation here is a picture of No.1338, an attractive little engine that was associated with the town for many years. It was one of two engines of the same design built by Kitson & Co. for the Cardiff Railway in 1898 and weighed a mere 25tons 10cwt; its sister locomotive was scrapped as long ago as 1932. It was nominally allocated to Taunton depot in 1943 but was actually based at Bridgwater sub-shed for shunting the docks, a chore it performed until June 1960, by which time commercial shipping there was a pale shadow of former years. No.1338 was then moved to Swansea docks and remained in BR service until withdrawn in September 1963. This picture was taken at Bridgwater docks on 18th December 1959. This dainty little locomotive survives in preservation and, at the time of writing, is located at the Great Western Society's Didcot depot. *Colour-Rail*

YATTON TO CLEVEDON

The 3½ miles-long Yatton to Clevedon branch was originally opened as a broad gauge line on 28th July 1847. Optimistically, the formation was built with doubling at a later date in mind but this was never justified by traffic levels. The branch was converted to standard gauge in 1879. Clevedon branch auto trains used a bay platform on the up side of Yatton station and here 1400 Class 0-4-2T No.1463 is depicted waiting to depart on 29th August 1959. Three of these locomotives were allocated to Bristol (Bath Road) shed for the branch, one engine being sub-shedded at Yatton for a week at a time during which it amassed an aggregate of 1,400 miles. There was a small engine shed at Yatton which was accessed solely from the bay used by branch trains. *David Soggee*

The charming little branch terminus at Clevedon, showing the auto train seen in the previous picture waiting at the platform. For many years the line was the preserve of a GWR steam rail-motor until auto trains took over. The branch was dieselised from 8th August 1960, with services being formed of a diesel multiple unit from that date. The station had one long platform with a run round loop and an overall roof at the buffer stop end. There was also a goods yard which had four sidings, one of these connecting with the nearby Weston, Clevedon & Portishead Light Railway. Latterly the branch was worked on the 'one engine in steam' principle, but the original B&ER railway signal box survived as a ground frame. In the early 1960s there was a frequent service of 30 return trains each weekday, but despite this lavish pattern the line was deemed to be uneconomic, closing from 3rd October 1966.
David Soggee

TAUNTON TO YEOVIL

The Bristol & Exeter Railway was authorised by an Act of Parliament in 1845 to construct a broad gauge, single track line from Taunton to Yeovil. The route ran from Durston Junction, on the Taunton to Bristol main line, to Hendford which was situated just outside Yeovil. It should be noted that, at the time, the principal route from the West Country to London was via Bristol, the more direct line via Castle Cary not being constructed until many years later. Work on the Yeovil branch commenced in 1847 but progress was slow due to the B&ER giving priority to other projects, and opening to Hendford was delayed until October 1853. The Wiltshire, Somerset & Weymouth Railway opened its line from Frome to Yeovil (Pen Mill) on 1st September 1856 and the line from Taunton was extended enabling the two routes to be linked. LSWR trains from Sherborne also ran to Hendford for a very brief period. The Taunton to Yeovil line was converted to standard gauge in 1879. Like so many rural lines, the route's traffic was eroded by the growth in private motoring and it eventually closed on 15th June 1964, but goods traffic at the Yeovil end continued until May 1968. Here, 5700 Class pannier tank locomotive No.9718 pauses at Langport West on 24th June 1961 after arrival with the 12.35pm from Taunton. This train then waited for 28 minutes, during which time it was crossed by a train travelling in the opposite direction, before continuing to Yeovil. The Taunton-bound train was due away from Langport West at 1.11pm so the reason for the extended wait (from 12.55pm to 1.23pm) is something of a mystery and, needless to say, a totally infuriating experience for through passengers! *John Langford*

A Taunton to Yeovil train, with Class 4575 2-6-2T No.4593 in charge, arrives at Martock on 30th May 1964. Despite the fact that withdrawal of the passenger service was only a few weeks away a fair number of passengers are waiting on the platform: perhaps they were all going for a farewell trip! An interesting feature of Martock station was the staggered platforms, this shot being taken from the footbridge which connected them. There was a small goods yard here and, at the southern end of the station, a level crossing controlled by an adjacent signal box. *Roy Hobbs*

The 4.00pm Yeovil to Taunton train, headed by BR Standard Class 4MT 4-6-0 No.75003, was recorded entering Montacute station on 11th April 1964. The facilities here were modest, consisting of a single platform plus a tiny goods yard and shed, which is just discernible in the background. Goods traffic was withdrawn from 30th September 1963. Latterly the signal box was only used during shunting operations and is reported to have been 'switched out' since about 1930. The Southern Region became responsible for the Langport West to Yeovil section in 1950, hence the somewhat incongruous green painted station signs. Note the improvised station lighting! *Hugh Ballantyne*

A train from Taunton, hauled by BR Standard Class 3MT 2-6-2T No.82044, approaches Hendford Halt on a sunny day in September 1963. There was considerable industrial development in this area as evidenced here by the factories in the picture. No.82044 was the last of 45 locomotives designed and built at Swindon Works for light passenger work mainly on the Western and Southern regions. The design was based on the GWR 6100 Class and the BR Standard engines had almost identical boilers. The first example appeared in April 1952 while No.82044 did not enter service until August 1955, the long period being due to the fact that the locomotives were constructed in two distinct batches. *Alan Reeve*

A scene at Hendford Halt in September 1963 showing GWR pannier tank locomotive No.4622 apparently preparing to shunt a long freight train into Hendford goods yard, which was located on the other side of the road bridge from where the shot was taken. An unidentified Maunsell 'Mogul', which had presumably brought in the freight train, stands on the adjacent track. In the very earliest days of railways in this area Hendford was the terminus of the broad gauge line from Taunton, the original station being located on a different site to that seen here, closer to Yeovil. There was even an engine shed here for a brief period until the line was extended to Yeovil (Pen Mill) in 1857, as previously mentioned. Hendford Halt was opened on 2nd May 1932 to serve the expanding industrial district. *Alan Reeve*

A general view of the layout at the western end of Yeovil Town station and engine shed, photographed on 11th July 1964. Construction of the station, which opened on 1st June 1861, was a joint venture between the B&ER and LSWR. The main building was a large symmetrical structure with a fine frontage while most of the platform area was covered by a bright and lofty train shed, built using cast iron components. The latter was removed in the 1930s and replaced by Southern Railway-style platform canopies largely constructed of steel. The station was always a curious mix of GWR and Southern practice and at one time it was maintained by the Southern Railway while the signalling was the responsibility of the GWR. For a long period the station was also divided operationally into GWR and Southern sections, the former apparently being restricted to the through line to Pen Mill station and a mere three sidings! Following the closure of the Taunton line in mid-1964 Yeovil Town station experienced a rapid decline with regular steam workings being ousted by diesels within a year, although the shed remained in use for stabling modern traction. The last freight trains ran in 1968 and during the following year the station area saw use as a reception area for track materials lifted during the singling of the Castle Cary to Dorchester route. The final blow came in 1970 when the town council sanctioned the demolition of the imposing station building and Town station, which had been by far the nearest of Yeovil's three stations to the town centre, was no more. *Michael Chown*

After leaving Yeovil Town, trains bound for Pen Mill station traversed a single track link between the two stations which ran alongside an area of high ground separating the line from the town centre. This doubtless gave unwary passengers the misleading impression they were passing through a rural area whereas, actually, they were less than half a mile from Yeovil town centre! Here, a train from Taunton, hauled by rather dirty BR Standard Class 3MT No.82042, heads for Pen Mill station in May 1964. *Roy Hobbs*

The standard gauge branch of the LSWR to Chard was opened on 8th May 1863 and was the first railway to reach that town. It diverged from the main Salisbury to Exeter line at Chard Junction station (previously known as Chard Road) and ran to a terminus known as Chard Town. The line was promoted by the independent Chard Railway Company but soon after construction had commenced they sold out to the LSWR who operated the branch from the outset and wound up the local company in 1864. The passenger service took the form of a shuttle service between the Junction and Town stations. The line from Chard to Taunton was also promoted by a purely local company, the Chard & Taunton Railway, who obtained an Act of Parliament in 1861, but the B&ER took control of the company in 1863 and started construction of its broad gauge route during the following year, the line opening in September 1866. Its line left the Taunton to Bristol main line (the line to Westbury was not built until much later) at Creech Junction and terminated in Chard at a site half a mile north of the LSWR's branch. On 26th November 1866 the LSWR opened a spur to link the two separate termini at Chard, the B&ER station being henceforth known as Chard Joint station (renamed Chard Central in 1949), but through working was not possible until the broad gauge line was converted to standard gauge in 1891. This development encouraged the two companies to work together and in 1916 the LSWR closed Chard Town station and all passenger traffic was concentrated on the Joint station. The entire branch was closed temporarily due to a fuel crisis in 1951 and after years of decline the branch was closed permanently to passenger traffic on 10th September 1962. A Taunton to Chard Central train, headed by 5700 Class 0-6-0PT No.4663, leaves Thornfalcon station some time during the summer of 1960. The modest station depicted here was brought into use in 1871, five years after this section of the branch was opened, and was initially named 'Thorn'. It was renamed Thornfalcon on 1st January 1902. The layout consisted of a single platform and a loop which ran around the back of the platform to give access to a small goods yard. The layout was controlled by a tiny signal box on the platform but this fell victim to early economy measures and was closed prior to the First World War. *Colour-Rail*

The sun is shining brightly, the locomotive is emitting clouds of black smoke and 'blowing off' as it trundles along, whilst the squat tunnel mouth and backdrop of trees just coming into leaf provide a branch line idyll. This shot shows the 2.50pm Taunton to Chard train approaching Hatch station behind BR Standard Class 3MT No.82044 on 28th April 1962, a lovely spring day. Hatch tunnel was 154 yards-long and the Brunel-style station had a goods loop but only one platform so it was not possible for passenger trains to cross there. *Roy Patterson*

A scene at Ilminster station on 18th August 1962 showing the 4.30pm Taunton to Chard Central train arriving with GWR pannier tank locomotive No.4622 in charge. The station here consisted of a single platform with a goods loop which enabled a passenger train to cross a goods working or two goods trains to cross. The loop, however, was not signalled for use by trains carrying passengers. The very last passenger train to serve Ilminster was the 9.30pm Chard Central to Taunton, hauled by locomotive No.4663, on 8th September 1962. *Alan Chandler*

A further view of Ilminster looking towards Taunton, in which the rather fine, original Bristol & Exeter Railway station buildings are prominent. On the left of the picture is the signal box with the goods yard behind. The signal box here remained in sporadic use until the line north of Chard was closed to goods traffic in 1964. Like other stations on the Chard branch Ilminster was situated some distance from the town centre which probably deterred all but the most determined travellers. This photograph was taken on 25th June 1961. *John Langford*

Stations do not come much smaller than this! The inter wars years saw two minor additions to the branch's passenger facilities, the opening of halts at Ilton, between Hatch (the station south of Thornfalcon) and Ilminster, plus Donyatt, between Ilminster and Chard. The former was brought into use on 26th May 1928 while the latter was opened on 5th May of the same year. Donyatt Halt, seen here on 28th April 1962 with No.4673 approaching with the 4.40pm *ex*-Taunton, was a very simple construction, the platform consisting of a timber facing with earth infill behind. Donyatt at least had the luxury of a rudimentary wooden shelter, unlike Ilton where (at least in recent years) no protection from the elements was provided. Latterly Ilton consisted of pre-cast concrete sections and it is thought it may have been 'modernised' during the period the Chard branch was under SR control in the 1950s.
Roy Patterson

A really busy scene, at least by the modest standards of the Chard branch, at Chard Central on 24th June 1961. The 5.4pm Chard Junction to Taunton train, made up of two coaches and a van, makes a brisk getaway behind 5700 Class pannier tank locomotive No.4644, while 7400 Class No.7436 simmers quietly in the siding with the stock of the 5.30pm to Chard Junction. The train service on the branch was designed to provide main line connections at either Taunton or Chard Junction and was operated, in effect, as two separate lines with an end-on junction at Chard Central. This method of operation continued until the end so, for example, passengers on the 4.30pm from Taunton to Chard Central were obliged to wait 20 minutes at Chard before an onward connection, the 5.30pm train to Chard Junction (depicted here), departed southwards. Other 'connections' at Chard involved waits of more than an hour! The 5.4pm *ex*-Chard Junction, which also features in this shot, was one of only three trains advertised as providing a through service to Taunton. Two other trains started at Chard Central, one of which had a good connection from Chard Junction but the other involved a 40 minute wait!
John Langford

A train to Chard Junction, hauled by 7400 Class 0-6-0PT No.7436, leaves Chard Central on 3rd August 1961. Note that, in addition to the usual two-coach set, a milk tank wagon and a horsebox are also formed in the train. The GWR built signal boxes at each end of the station, Chard North box opening in 1892 while the South signal box was brought into use four years later. The latter was closed as early as 1st January 1917 and thereafter the North box controlled the entire station. Despite years of operation under the jurisdiction of the GWR, towards the end the branch had a number of upper quadrant 'Southern' signals on rail-built posts, which had presumably replaced lower quadrant GWR signals during the period the SR was in control between 1950 and 1958. *Colour-Rail*

No.7436 is seen again, this time simmering at Chard Central's grassy platform after arrival with the 4.27pm from Taunton on 24th June 1961. Note the station's very gloomy interior and Royal Mail van on the platform. The overgrown area on the left was the site of the LSWR's bay platform which was filled in after 1927. *John Langford*

A portrait of the rather fine Chard Central station taken from the approach road. Brunel's original B&ER station building survived until closure although latterly it was extremely neglected. Right to the end passengers were reminded of the station's beginnings by the words 'Bristol & Exeter Railway Booking Office' emblazoned above a doorway. For a short period, when the station was served by both standard and broad gauge trains, the former used a bay platform at the southern end of the station while broad gauge services from Taunton ran into a bay at the northern end. It is probable that the southernmost bay was taken out of use in 1917 and it was removed altogether in 1927. Both companies had sidings to a canal basin, situated north of the station, and to reach this the LSWR ran over a dual gauge track that ran through the station: this line also gave access to a dual gauge turntable. The GWR also had its own engine shed but this was closed in 1924. The GWR was alarmed by the possibility of an LSWR incursion into Taunton and because of this gauge conversion of the Chard branch was delayed until the very end of the broad gauge era, re-gauging being deferred until 1891. This picture was also taken on 24th June 1961, a beautiful summer's day. *John Langford*

The first station in Chard was, as previously mentioned, the LSWR's Chard Town, opened on 8th May 1863. The station had a single platform, a small goods yard with a goods shed, an engine shed and a signal box, and services took the form of a shuttle to and from Chard Junction. The premises had a short existence as a passenger station, being converted to goods only use in 1916 following cooperation between the GWR and LSWR which resulted in services being concentrated on Chard Joint station. The signal box was shut at the same time and replaced by a two-lever ground frame which controlled the connection to the 'main' line. The engine shed was taken out of use in about 1920 and subsequently removed. Known locally in its early years as the 'tin station', the former Chard Town is seen here on 28th April 1962. *Roy Patterson*

A view of the Chard branch platform at Chard Junction station on 3rd September 1962, exactly a week before closure of the branch. 5700 Class 0-6-0PT No.4663 waits patiently at the platform while staff attend to mailbags. The 'main line' goods yard and shed are visible on the left. The line to Chard Central curved away very sharply and can just be discerned between the permanent way hut and the mineral wagon. The principal, main line, part of Chard Junction, where the station buildings were situated, is out of sight on the left of the shot and separated from the branch platform by the station approach road. The branch platform looked as though it had been built by an alien railway company and banished to a corner of the station whereas, in fact, it was a LSWR branch from the start. Passenger trains to and from Chard Central ran as 'mixed' whenever needed and at Chard Junction this required some interesting manoeuvres. Passengers on mixed trains starting there would board the train first which would then reverse into an adjacent siding to pick up the wagons and brake van. *Colour-Rail*

A further illustration of the Chard branch platform at Chard Junction station which, as previously stated, was situated 'across the road' from the main line part of the station. This shows decidedly dirty pannier tank engine No.9663 waiting to leave for Chard Central in September 1960. Note the Chard Road Hotel in the background, a reminder of bygone days when the station was known as Chard Road. The single coach forming the train is a former slip coach – note it has guard's brake vans at both ends – in chocolate and cream livery. Slip coaches were detached from express trains at speed and enabled intermediate stations to be served (for alighting passengers only) without stopping the main train. Each individual slip coach conveyed its own guard who took charge of the braking, once the coach had been detached, in order to ensure it came to rest at the platform. One of the drawbacks of travelling in a slip coach was its isolation from the rest of the train, which meant that passengers were unable to reach the restaurant car. The GWR was a prolific user of this type of operation and at one time as many as seventy-nine slips were advertised at twenty-four different locations. Some trains 'slipped' as many as three times, such as the 'Cornish Riviera Express' at Westbury, Taunton and Exeter. The last slip of all involved the 5.10pm Paddington to Wolverhampton which slipped a coach at Bicester on 9th September 1960, after which, one might say, the practice slipped into history. *Colour-Rail*

TAUNTON TO MINEHEAD

The branch from Taunton (Norton Fitzwarren) to Minehead was built in two separate stages, the first section being from the main line junction to Watchet whilst the second stretch was from there to the attractive seaside resort of Minehead. The entire line was originally built to the broad gauge. Promoted by the West Somerset Railway, the route as far as Watchet was authorised by an Act of Parliament obtained in 1857 and the traditional ceremony of cutting the first sod took place near Crowcombe on 7th April 1859. The first trains ran on 31st March 1862 which was a day of great rejoicing, especially in Watchet where a triumphal arch had been erected at the station entrance. At this time the local fishing industries at nearby Minehead were in steep decline and the harbour was suffering from silting. It was, however, becoming fashionable for people to spend time at the seaside for its health giving properties plus socialising, and the local landowners saw the development of the tourist trade as the town's salvation vowing to connect Minehead with the expanding railway system. Unfortunately, the 1866 financial crash, which made the raising of money almost impossible, delayed matters but on 29th June 1871 the Minehead Railway's plans for an extension from Watchet received the Royal Assent. The first train left Minehead amid great celebration at 6.00am on 16th July 1874. The complete route was converted to standard gauge in 1882. The first sod, as previously mentioned, was cut near Crowcombe station, which is seen here is this early 1960s picture. This is the summit of the line and the lowest crossing point between the Quantock and Brendon hills. When the station opened a new, 650 yards-long roadway was laid from the nearby country lanes to provide access. Expectations of goods traffic were low so the station was provided only with a short loading siding at the Minehead end of the premises. The signal box and loop were added in about 1883 whilst an extra platform on the down side was commissioned in November 1891. Further improvements were carried out in 1934. *Colour-Rail*

Regrettably many of the lines featured in this book have long since been consigned to history, a situation that could, perhaps, have been avoided had it not been for BR's lamentable failure to promote them. The Taunton to Minehead line, for example, runs through some of the loveliest countryside in Great Britain, bordering the outstanding Quantock Hills for mile after mile before it reaches the shores of the Bristol Channel. Pasengers on board northbound trains obtained their first glimpse of the sea just before Watchet was reached and in this shot an unidentified 2-6-2T is seen running down the bank into Watchet on 6th August 1961. *Roy Denison*

Hauling a six-coach rake of BR Standard coaches, two of which are in carmine and cream livery, 2-6-2T No.4128 nears Watchet with a Minehead-bound working on 30th July 1961. The train is rounding the curve at the approach to Doniford bridge where Doniford Halt is now located. Note that the hay in the field adjoining the line has been arranged into stooks, a traditional farming practice that, regrettably, has long been consigned to history. *David Soggee*

Opposite: The small industrial town of Watchet – which seems somewhat out of place in rural West Somerset – was the branch terminus for more than 12 years until the extension to Minehead opened in 1874. The station consists of a single stone platform and station building plus a goods shed. Originally, when Watchet was 'the end of the line' locomotives were serviced at a small engine shed, where there was a turntable plus coal and watering facilities, but most of this equipment was later moved to Minehead. Watchet station was the second busiest on the branch after Minehead and even in 1959 (the last year for which figures are available) 32,000 tickets were sold. Here a Taunton-bound train awaits departure from Watchet on 30th July 1961. Govier's Lane foot crossing, visible beyond the locomotive, was for many years a constant source of dispute between the railway authorities and local council who considered that visibility was poor in both directions due to the crossing being situated on a curve. Between 1888 and 1932 there were three fatalities involving pedestrians, but the GWR refused to construct the bridge or subway demanded by the council. An automatic warning bell was, however, installed in 1909. *David Soggee*

A further photograph of Watchet station this time looking towards Minehead. The train depicted is the one seen in the previous picture. Note the rather dainty lamp standard on the left. The building partly visible in the middle of the shot is the goods shed (which still exists) while on the right can be seen an additional shed that was constructed when there was a shortage of covered goods accommodation. This open sided shed was erected in 1905 primarily to store paper pulp for a nearby mill, but it was later put to more general use by local coal merchants. The down distant signal, visible above the third coach of the train, was controlled by Kentsford signal box (between Watchet and Washford), Watchet's own signal cabin having been taken out of use way back in 1926. *David Soggee*

A general view of the railway installations at Watchet showing the station on the left and harbour, where it is clearly low tide! The lofty building in the centre of the picture is the former Wesleyan chapel that was erected in 1871, whilst an array of buildings along the esplanade is also prominent, including the erstwhile Ritz cinema. The harbour sidings at Watchet were notoriously difficult to work, the only access being via the scissors crossover and very short headshunt near the goods shed. This meant that all trains had to be divided into very small portions before they could be moved onto the dockside. In addition movement around the sidings was hampered by the need to move trucks individually on wagon turntables – an extremely inconvenient and time consuming operation. This picture was also taken on 30th July 1961. *David Soggee*

'Oh, I do like to be beside the seaside'. It may not be apparent from this picture, but when trains reached Blue Anchor they were certainly beside the seaside, the station being almost on the beach! Here, Large Prairie No.4157 pauses with an unidentified Minehead-bound working in May 1960, with the sea not far away on the left. Like other stations on the branch, Blue Anchor station underwent considerable improvement over the years, perhaps the most dramatic enhancement taking place in April 1904 when the signal box and loop were opened. The platforms and loop were extended in 1934. The tiny goods yard there, which consisted of just one siding, was opened for business in April 1913 but traffic was always rather thin and Blue Anchor held the unenviable position as the station on the branch handling the smallest amount of goods traffic. Its close proximity to the sea made Blue Anchor the ideal site for a camping coach and in 1934 it became one of the first stations on the GWR to have this facility. *Colour-Rail*

A shaft of sunlight beautifully illuminates Minehead station as Collett 6100 Class 2-6-2T No.6157 runs round its train after arrival from Taunton on 30th July 1961. The station seems to be almost totally deserted in contrast to today's busy scenes. Note the collection of vintage vehicles on the land adjacent to the line. Unlike many other stations that were poorly situated in relation to their town centres, Minehead station could not have been in a better position. It was built just a few yards from the sea at the end of The Avenue, a fine, wide thoroughfare mostly lined with semi-detached villas, and is ideally sited in the town which advertises itself as the 'Gateway to Exmoor'. The somewhat basic original terminus soon started to be overwhelmed as Minehead established itself as a fashionable watering place for the well-off and grandiose plans were made in 1903 to enlarge the premises. These came to nothing, however, apart from the construction of a new platform and signal box in 1905. In 1910 a new 45 foot-long turntable was provided next to the small engine shed. The main station building was enlarged in 1923, but another eleven years elapsed before the next substantial improvement took place. In 1934 major work was carried out as part of the general upgrade of facilities along the branch, the most noticeable change, perhaps, being the lengthening of the platforms from 750 to 1,250 feet and doubling of the track as far as Dunster, which allowed one train to leave Minehead whilst another was approaching. Minehead lost its freight facilities in July 1964 while the signal box closed in 1966. BR vacated the station in 1971 upon withdrawal of the service, but that, of course, was not entirely the end of the story. *David Soggee*

Thanks to the untiring efforts and remarkable commitment of many railway enthusiasts the Taunton to Minehead line survived, after a shaky start, to become one of the most successful preserved railways in Great Britain. Today it is known once again as the West Somerset Railway and evocative scenes such as that depicted here can still be seen at Minehead station. The picture shows a train bound for Taunton waiting to depart, under the watchful eye of the stationmaster, on 5th September 1962 with 4575 Class 2-6-2T No.5563 in charge. This locomotive was a Swindon product (naturally!) that dated from December 1928 and it lasted in service until September 1964. The wooded slopes of North Hill form the backdrop. *Colour-Rail*

TAUNTON TO BARNSTAPLE

The cross-country Taunton to Barnstaple line weaved its way along the southern slopes of Exmoor passing through some of the loveliest rural landscapes of any route featured in this book. It was characterised by its string of immaculately kept country stations serving no more than small villages or hamlets. Unfortunately, the line served no large intermediate settlements, the only places of any size being Dulverton and South Molton, but the stations at both of those locations were some distance from the town centre. The route was originally broad gauge and opened throughout on 1st November 1873; it was converted to standard gauge in 1881. The first station on the branch after Taunton was Milverton which, despite its apparently modern goods shed, still creates a charming scene in this view (looking eastwards) taken on 8th June 1963. *Roy Patterson*

On summer Saturdays the Taunton to Barnstaple line really came to life because a number of heavy holiday trains from London, the Midlands and the north of England were routed this way. But the line always 'rested' on a Sunday, there being no timetabled service at any time of the year. This picture, however, depicts an ordinary local train, these latterly being the preserve of Churchward 'Moguls'. Here, a nicely cleaned No.7326 is seen near Wiveliscombe with a Barnstaple to Taunton train on 15th September 1962. Originally constructed as 9300 Class No.9304 in February 1932, No.7326 was renumbered in June 1958 and subsequently lasted in service until September 1963. *John Beckett*

Wiveliscombe was a delightfully quiet country station situated on a very tight curve where, it has to be admitted, the station staff had plenty of time to tend the roses and trim the hedges between trains. The prominent running-in board, traditional 'Gentlemen' sign with a 'hand' pointing towards the door and barrows on the platforms all add to the charm of the picture. Curiously, there were at least three completely different styles of gas lamp standard at Wiveliscombe. *Roy Patterson*

A Taunton to Barnstaple train, with 4300 Class 2-6-0 No.7337 in charge, leaves Dulverton on 28th September 1963. Much of the line west of Taunton was in the county of Devon and therefore outside the scope of this album, but just before Dulverton station was reached it crossed the county boundary once again and found itself back in Somerset. Dulverton was the junction for the delightful Exe Valley Line and by far the most important station on the Taunton to Barnstaple route. It suffered, however, due to its location being more than two miles away from the town, so passengers without their own transport were faced with the stark choice of a long walk or spending a small fortune on a taxi. In its heyday Dulverton station was kept in immaculate condition. The staff took an immense pride in their station and ensured it was always a joy to behold. But it was all to no avail and it must have been a heartbreaking experience when the Exe Valley Line was closed in October 1963 followed almost exactly three years later by the Taunton to Barnstaple line. *Alan Jarvis*